Knots

Here are the knots that will become your mainstay! Some of these ar[e]
them in every project. Some you will use less often but you will find the[m]

Overhand Knot

Friendship Knot

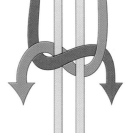

Half Knot - *Twist*

Half Hitch - *Twist Knot*

Half Hitch - *Double Knot*

Square Knot - *part 1 and part 2*

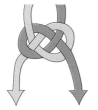

Josephine Knot

Bauble Knot

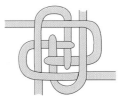

Knotted Cross

Hemp is preferred to other cords for jewelry because it knots easily and holds knots without glue.

Size of Hemp Cord

1/2 to 1 mm - 20#
1 to 2 mm - 48#
3 mm - 170#

————————— 1 mm

————————— 2 mm

————————— 3 mm

Bead Size -
Any size bead you want to wear is fine. You must be sure the hemp cord you are using will go through the hole easily. Also, beads are often added onto two cords.

The 5 Strand Bracelet on page 14 shows a technique for using a bead that only one cord will pass through.

Meaning of Bead Colors

YELLOW - *"I gaze at you as a flower gazes at the sun."*
GREEN - *"Like a new blade of grass, my love for you is green and growing."*
BLACK - *"Your absence deprives the noonday of light."*
BLUE - *"Our love is serene as the cloudless sky when the storm has passed."*
ORANGE - *"I bask in your radiance as a sunflower warms to the sun."*

How To Start

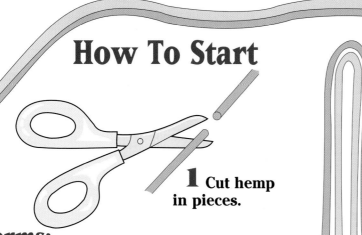

1 Cut hemp in pieces.

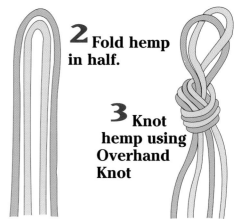

2 Fold hemp in half.

3 Knot hemp using Overhand Knot

Terms:

Add Beads - Always thread beads onto the filler cords, unless the instructions are different.

Fold Cord in Half - Find the center of each cord by folding it in half, so that both ends of each cord are the same length.

Knotting Cords - Longer cords will be used to tie the knots. Usually you will tie over/around filler cords. Bring the knotting cords to the outside (left & right side) of the work after the beginning knot is completed or an end clamp is attached.

Filler Cords - Shorter cords you will knot around. Beads will usually be strung onto these cords.

Basic Tips:

Tightening Knots - For a strong ending knot, tighten each cord individually. If possible use pliers to pull cords tight for the ending knots.

Running out of cord - Sometimes you can switch the remaining filler cord with the knotting cord, and get a few more knots. Switching filler cord will show a little, so hide the change in a bead or in the middle of a knot, if possible. Use Tacky glue when needed.

How To Measure:

Knotting cords should be 5 to 6 times as long as the finished piece, if you are using close Square Knots or Half Knot Twist, or any very dense knot. The more spaces or beads in the piece, the shorter the knotting cords can be. Also, if you knot tightly, you will need more cord; if you knot loosely, you will use less cord. It is always better to have too much cord, rather than too little! Hemp is not expensive, and you can always make keychains to give as gifts from your 'leftovers'.

Filler Cords will need to be long enough for you to tie your ending knot easily.

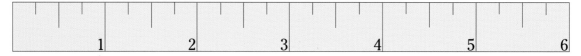

Closures:

Attach end clamps such as 'squeeze clamps' to beginning and ending cords. Dot cords with glue for a more secure hold.

Attach jump rings and/or eye rings to squeeze clamps with needle or chain nose pliers.

Incorrect way to open jump ring — opening ring wider.

Tools:

Use Needlenose pliers to attach end clamps to jump rings.

Correct way to open jump ring — side to side.

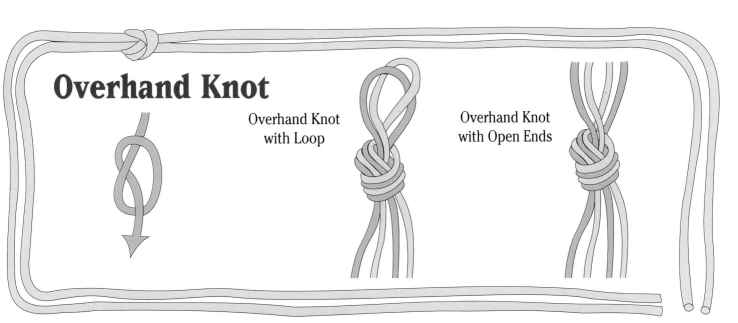

Overhand Knot

Overhand Knot
with Loop

Overhand Knot
with Open Ends

Two Color Overhand Knot Anklet

MATERIALS:
- One 60" piece of 2mm Natural hemp
- One 60" piece of 1mm Navy hemp

INSTRUCTIONS:

1 Fold cords in half; tie an Overhand Knot, leaving a ½" loop.

2 Using both cords, tie Overhand Knots, leaving a ⅜" space between knots. Continue to end of anklet.

3 Finish with a Double Overhand Knot (tie a second knot on top of the first knot). Trim the ends.

Three Color Overhand Knot Necklace

MATERIALS:
- One 80" piece of 1mm Red hemp
- One 80" piece of 1mm Natural hemp
- One 80" piece of 1mm Green hemp

INSTRUCTIONS:

1 Fold cords 4" from the end; tie 1 Overhand Knot, leaving a ½" loop. Dot knot with glue, pull tightly. Trim short ends.

2 With all 3 cords, tie Overhand Knots, leaving about ¾" of space between knots to the end of necklace.

3 Finish with a Double Overhand Knot (tie a second knot on top of the first knot). Trim the ends.

Signs of the Times Choker

MATERIALS:
- Two 30" pieces of 1mm Natural hemp
- Two square wooden flower beads
- One each square wooden beads with peace sign, yin-yang symbol, and happy face

INSTRUCTIONS:

1 Fold cords in half; tie an Overhand Knot, leaving a ½" loop.

2 Separate into 2 groups of two cords. Leave a ¾" space, tie an Overhand Knot in each group.

3 Leave a ¾" space, tie an Overhand Knot with the two center cords. Repeat pattern two more times.

4 Repeat Step 2. Add a bead in place of Step 3. Repeat Step 2. Continue adding beads and repeating Step 2 until all beads are added.

5 Repeat Steps 2 and 3 three times, then end with another Step 2. Tie a Double Overhand Knot (tie a second knot on top of the first knot). Trim the ends.

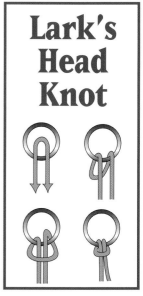

Three Bead Pendant Necklace

MATERIALS:
- Four 70" pieces of 1mm Natural hemp
- Four barrel beads, ½" long

INSTRUCTIONS:

1 Find the center of 2 cords; mount them onto a barrel bead with a Lark's Head Knot. Do not tighten the knot. Thread the 2 remaining cords through the back of the Lark's Head Knot. Even up the ends, tighten the knot.

2 Tie an Overhand Knot with all cords. Separate into 2 groups of 4 cords each. With one group, tie an Overhand Knot, leaving a 2" space. Add bead. Tie an Overhand Knot. Tie 2 more Overhand Knots, spacing them 2" apart. Repeat with the other group of cords.

3 On one end of the necklace, tie an Overhand Knot 2" from the last knot, skip 1", tie an Overhand Knot. Trim the ends.

4 On the other end, string a barrel bead onto all cords. Position the bead sideways, tie an Overhand Knot, spaced 2" from the last knot. Trim the ends.

Lark's Head Knot

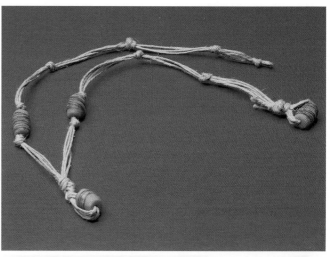

Friendship Knot

The Horizontal Wrap

The Diagonal Wrap

Knot around the left cord two times.

Knot around the center cord two times.

Knot around the third cord two times.

Friendship Hemp Bracelet in Natural & Black

MATERIALS:
- Two 110" pieces of 2mm Natural hemp
- Two 110" pieces of 2mm Black hemp

INSTRUCTIONS:

Note: The two Black cords are treated as one.

1 Fold the cords in half; tie an Overhand Knot, leaving a ½" loop. Arrange colors left to right with all the Natural cords first, then Black. Tape or pin the top of bracelet to work surface.

2 Using the first cord on the left, tie a knot over the next strand. Hold the second cord taut, and pull up on the first cord to tighten the knot.
Make a second knot next to the first knot, forming a Friendship Knot. Use the first cord to tie a pair of Friendship Knots on each remaining cord across the row. The first cord on the left side becomes the last cord on the right side.

3 Repeat the knotting sequence, knotting the left strand over all cords, to desired length of bracelet.

4 Tie an Overhand Knot with all cords, then separate into two groups. Braid each group for at least 3", and finish with an Overhand Knot. Trim the ends.

Three Strand Braid

Half Knot - Twist

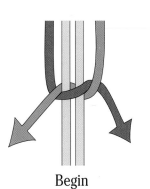

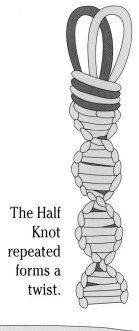

Begin

Repeat

The Half
Knot
repeated
forms a
twist.

Arrowhead Charm Choker

MATERIALS:
- One 180" piece of 1mm Natural hemp for knotting cord
- One 45" piece of 1mm Natural hemp for filler cord
- Two ⅝" Turquoise beads
- One Silver Arrowhead Charm
- Two large end clamps
- One clasp set
- Three jump rings

INSTRUCTIONS:

1 Fold cords in half; attach an end clamp.

2 Tie Half Knots for 7"; add a bead. Tie Half Knots for 1"; add a bead. Tie Half Knots for 7".

3 Bundle the cords, dot with glue. Attach an end clamp around these cords. Attach a clasp set to the end clamps with jump rings. Attach an Arrowhead charm to the center of the choker with a jump ring.

Twist Bracelet with Large Green & Blue Beads

MATERIALS:
- One 72" piece of 1mm Natural hemp for knotting cord
- One 20" piece of 1mm Natural hemp for filler cord
- Two round ½" green beads
- Two round ½" blue beads
- Two end clamps
- One clasp set
- Two jump rings

INSTRUCTIONS:

1 Fold cords in half; attach an end clamp.

2 Tie Half Knots for 1"; add a blue bead. Repeat, adding a green bead. Repeat, adding a blue bead. Repeat, adding a green bead. Tie Half Knots for 1".

3 Attach an end clamp. Trim ends. Attach a clasp set to end clamps.

Flower Charm Necklace

MATERIALS:
- One 160" piece of 1mm Natural hemp for knotting cord
- One 35" piece of 1mm Natural hemp for filler cord
- Two gold ⅜" cylinder beads
- Two gold ⅜" round beads
- One gold Flower charm
- One clasp set
- Three jump rings

INSTRUCTIONS:

1 Fold cords in half; attach an end clamp.

2 Tie Half Knots for 3½", add a cylinder bead. Tie Half Knots for 2", add a round bead. Tie Half Knots for 2½", add a round bead. Tie Half Knots for 2", add a cylinder bead. Tie Half Knots for 3½".

3 Bundle cords together, dot with glue. Attach end clamp. Trim ends when dry. Attach Flower charm between round beads with jump ring. Attach clasp set to end clamps with jump rings.

Half Hitch - Twist

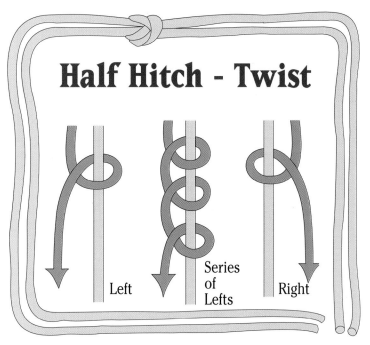

Left Series of Lefts Right

Half Hitch Twist in Natural & Black

MATERIALS:
- One 72" piece of 1mm of Natural hemp cord
- One 72" piece of 1mm of Black hemp cord

INSTRUCTIONS:

1 Fold the cords in half; tie an Overhand Knot, leaving a ½" loop.

2 Tie Half Hitches with Black cord over all cords for a distance of 1"; then tie Half Hitches with Natural cord over all cords for 1". Continue this pattern to the end of bracelet.

3 Tie all cords in a Double Overhand Knot (tie a second knot on top of the first knot) to finish. Trim the ends.

NOTE: When you repeat the Half Hitch Knot, it will cause the cord to "twist".

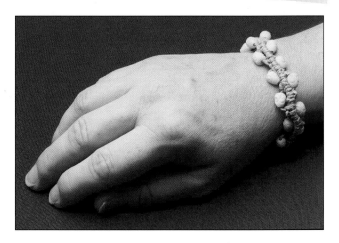

Beaded Half Hitch Bracelet

MATERIALS:
- One 120" piece of 1mm Natural hemp for knotting cord
- One 20" piece of 1mm Natural hemp for filler cord
- Fourteen small white beads, 5/16"
- Two end clamps
- One clasp set
- Two jump rings

INSTRUCTIONS:

1 Fold cords in half; attach an end clamp.

2 With left cord, tie 2 Half Hitch Double Knots. With right cord, tie 2 Half Hitch Double Knots. With left cord, tie 2 Half Hitch Double Knots.

3 String bead onto right cord, tie 2 Half Double Hitch Knots. String bead onto left cord, tie 2 Half Hitch Double Knots. Continue this pattern until all beads have been added. Repeat Step 2.

4 Bundle cords together, dot with glue. Attach an end clamp. Attach clasp set to end clamps with jump rings.

Half Hitch - Double Knot

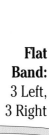

Single Knot:
1 Left,
1 Right

Double Knot:
2 Left,
2 Right

2 Left
Add bead,
2 Right
Add bead.

Flat Band:
3 Left,
3 Right

Natural & Black Necklace

MATERIALS:
• One 120" piece of 1mm Black hemp
• One 120" piece of 1mm Natural hemp

INSTRUCTIONS:

1 Put cords together; find a point 40" from the ends. Tie an Overhand Knot, leaving a ½" loop. Separate the colors: Natural on the left and Black on the right, with filler cords in the center. (Longer cords are knotting cords; shorter cords are filler cords).

2 Knot a Half Hitch - Double Knot **Flat Band** pattern (see above on page 11 - 3 left & 3 right) for the length of necklace. Keep knotting fairly tight, flattening the knotted band between your fingers if it starts to curl.

3 Finish with a Double Overhand Knot (tie a second knot on top of the first knot). Trim the ends.

Cross Charm Necklace

MATERIALS:
• Two 120" pieces of 1mm Natural hemp
• Four flat ⅜" diameter beads
• One gold cross charm
• Two large end clamps
• One clasp set
• Three jump rings

INSTRUCTIONS:

1 Fold cords together 40" from one end; attach an end clamp over the fold. *(Longer cords are knotting cords; shorter cords are filler cords.)*

2 Tie a Half Hitch - Double Knot **Flat Band** pattern (see above - 3 left & 3 right) for 4½"; add 2 beads. Tie a **Flat Band** pattern for 3"; add 2 beads. Tie a **Flat Band** pattern for 4½".

3 Bundle cords together, dot with glue. Attach an end clamp. Trim ends when dry. Attach a cross charm to the choker with a jump ring. Attach a clasp set to the end clamps with jump rings.

NOTE: This necklace is made with the same knotting pattern as the Natural & Black necklace. It will be simpler to knot if you practice in two colors first.

Square Knot

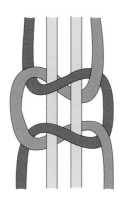

Part 1

Part 1
and
Part 2

Complete
Square
Knot

Sinnet
or
Series
of
Knots

Square Knot Necklace with a Large Green Bead

MATERIALS:
- One 160" piece of 2mm Natural hemp for knotting cord
- One 80" piece of 2mm Natural hemp for filler cord
- One large Green Bead 1½"
- Two 3⁄16" Blue Beads

INSTRUCTIONS:

1 Fold the cords in half; tie an Overhand Knot, leaving a ½" loop. Tie 22 Square Knots.

2 Add 1 small bead. Tie 1 Square Knot, add the large bead, tie 1 Square Knot. Add 1 small bead.

3 Tie 22 Square Knots. Finish with a Double Overhand Knot (tie a second knot on top of the first knot). Trim the ends.

Twist & Square Knot Anklet

MATERIALS:
- Two 120" pieces of 1mm Natural hemp for knotting cords
- Two 30" pieces of 1mm Natural hemp for filler cord
- Two small ¼" white beads

INSTRUCTIONS:

1 Fold the cords in half; tie an Overhand Knot, leaving a ½" loop.

2 Tie 7 Square Knots; add a bead. Tie 3 Square Knots.

3 Tie 3" of Half Knot Twists (see page 8). Tie Square Knots for 2". Tie Half Knot Twists for 3".

4 Add a bead, tie off with an Overhand Knot. Trim the ends.

'Slave' Anklet

MATERIALS:
- One 80" piece of 1mm Natural hemp for knotting cord
- One 45" piece of 1mm Natural hemp for filler cord
- One round ½" colorful Fimo clay bead
- Two round ⅜" colorful Fimo clay beads

INSTRUCTIONS:

1 Fold the cords in half; tie an Overhand Knot, leaving a 1" loop. Tie 1 Square Knot; add a small bead. Tie 3 Square Knots; add a small bead. Tie 5 Square Knots; add the large bead. Tie 2 Square Knots.

2 Leave a ½" space, tie a Square Knot. Repeat 11 times, or to fit your foot.

3 Finish with a 3/4" space, tie 1 Square Knot. Tie an Overhand Knot. Trim the ends.

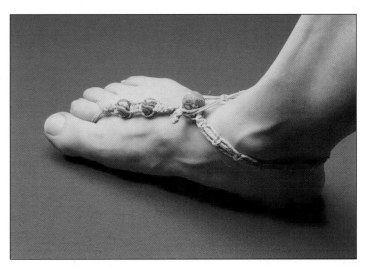

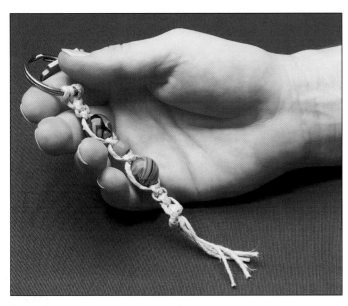

Square Knot Keychain

MATERIALS:
- One 24" piece of 2mm Natural hemp for knotting cord
- One 14" piece of 2mm Natural hemp for filler cord
- Two round ½" multicolor beads
- One ¼" blue pony bead
- One 1" key ring

INSTRUCTIONS:

1 Fold the cords in half; mount cords to the key ring with a Lark's Head Knot.

2 Tie 2 Square Knots, add a round bead. Tie 1 Square Knot, add the pony bead. Tie 1 Square Knot, add a round bead.

3 Tie 2 Square Knots. Tie an Overhand Knot. Trim the ends.

Lark's Head Knot

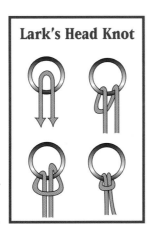

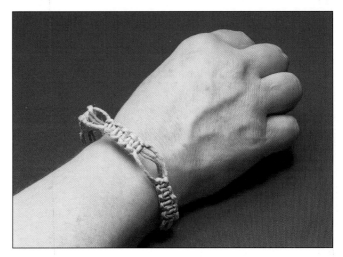

Simple Square Knot Bracelet

MATERIALS:
- One 70" piece of 2mm Natural hemp for knotting cord
- One 30" piece of 2mm Turquoise hemp for filler cord

INSTRUCTIONS:

1 Fold the knotting cord in half. Attach the filler cord with a Lark's Head Knot, leaving a ½" loop. Tie 5 Square Knots.

2 Leave a ½" space, tie 4 Square Knots. Repeat this pattern until you have 5 spaces with 4 Square Knots between each space. Tie 5 Square Knots after the last space.

3 Finish with a Double Overhand Knot (tie a second knot on top of the first knot). Trim the ends.

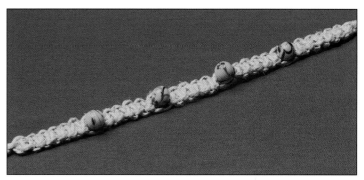

Lavender Bead Bracelet

MATERIALS:
- One 80" piece of 2mm Natural hemp for knotting cord
- One 30" piece of 2mm Natural hemp for filler cord
- Two Lavender tube beads, ¾" long

INSTRUCTIONS:

1 Fold the cords in half; tie an Overhand Knot, leaving a ½" loop. Tie 8 Square Knots. Leave a ½" space, tie 2 Square Knots.

2 Tie the first half of a Square Knot; add a bead, finish the Square Knot. Tie 2 Square Knots.

3 Leave a ½" space, tie 2 Square Knots. Repeat step 2. Repeat step 3.

4 Tie 8 Square Knots after the last space. Finish with a Double Overhand Knot (tie a second knot on top of the first knot). Trim the ends.

Melon Bead Necklace

MATERIALS:
- One 180" piece of 1mm Natural hemp for knotting cord
- One 60" piece of 1mm Natural hemp for filler cord
- Five ⅝" long melon shaped beads
- Two large end clamps
- One clasp set
- Two jump rings

INSTRUCTIONS:

1 Fold the knotting cord in half; attach one end clamp. Attach the filler cord to the knotting cord with an Overhand Knot. Tie 8 Square Knots; add a bead.

2 Tie 11 Square Knots; add a bead. Continue pattern of 11 Square Knots, add a bead until all beads are added. Tie 8 Square Knots after the last bead.

3 Bundle all cords together, dot with glue. Attach an end clamp. Trim when dry. Attach the clasp set to end clamps with jump rings.

Five Strand Bracelet with Yellow Beads

MATERIALS:
- One 96" piece of 2mm Natural hemp for knotting cord
- One 35" piece of 2mm Natural hemp for filler cord
- One 20" piece of 1mm Natural hemp for filler cord & beads
- Four ⅜" round beads
- One clasp set
- Two jump rings
- Two large end clamps

INSTRUCTIONS:

1 Fold knotting cords in half; put end of 1mm cord into fold. Attach end clamp around all cords.

2 Tie 6 Square Knots over all three filler cords.

3 Add a bead to the 1mm cord; tie 5 Square Knots. Continue to add a bead in this way between every 5 Square Knots, until all four beads have been added. Tie 6 Square Knots after the last bead.

4 Bundle cords together, attach end clamp. Trim ends. Attach clasp set to end clamps with jump rings.

Four Strand Alternating Square Knot

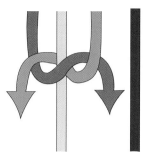

1st half of Knot   2nd half of Knot

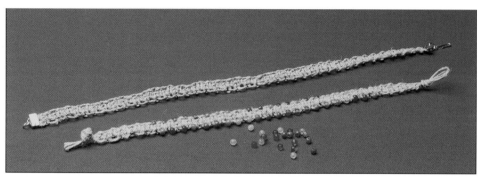

Four Strand - Quick Lacy Choker

MATERIALS:
- Two 80" pieces of 1mm Natural hemp
- One clasp set
- Two end clamps
- Two jump rings

INSTRUCTIONS:

1 Fold the cords in half; attach one end clamp.

2 Knot the entire choker in a Four Strand Alternating Knot pattern.

3 Bundle all cords together; dot with glue and attach an end clamp. Trim the ends when dry. Attach a clasp set to each end clamp with jump rings.

Four Strand - Rainbow Bead Choker

MATERIALS:
- Two 80" pieces of 1mm Natural hemp
- 45 small colored beads

INSTRUCTIONS:

1 Fold the cords in half; tie an Overhand Knot, leaving a ½" loop.

2 Knot in a Four Strand Alternating Square Knot pattern for 1". To begin adding beads: Continue this knotting pattern, but string a bead onto the outside cord before tying the next Square Knot. Arrange your beads colors like a rainbow, or in any pattern that pleases you. Repeat the 1" section without beads at the end.

3 Finish with a Double Overhand Knot (tie a second knot on top of the first knot). Trim the ends.

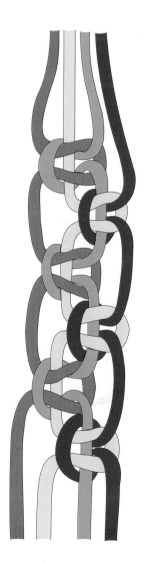

Four Strand
Alternating
Square Knot

Eight Strand Alternating Square Knot

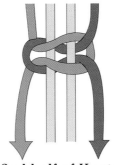
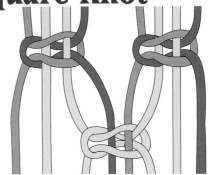

1st half of Knot   2nd half of Knot   Eight strand Alternating Square Knot

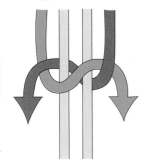
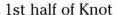

Eight Strand - Bracelet with Black & Multi Beads

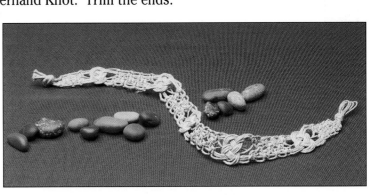

MATERIALS:
- Four 48" pieces of 1mm Natural hemp
- One multi-colored ½" round bead
- Two black/white ¼" round beads

INSTRUCTIONS:

1 Fold the cords in half; tie with an Overhand Knot, leaving a ½" loop.

2 Tie Alternating Square Knots for 2".

3 Add a black/white bead onto the center cords. Tie Alternating Square Knots for ½". Add a multi-colored bead onto the center cords. Tie Alternating Square Knots for ½". Add a black/white bead to the center cords. Tie Alternating Square Knots for 2".

4 Finish with a Double Overhand Knot. Trim the ends.

Alternating Square Knot Necklace with Josephine Knots

MATERIALS:
- Four 95" pieces of 1mm Natural hemp

INSTRUCTIONS:

1 Fold the cords in half; tie an Overhand Knot, leaving a ½" loop.

Alternating Square Knot Section: Divide the cords into 2 groups; tie 1 Square Knot with each group. Tie 1 Square Knot with the 4 center cords. Repeat 2 times, ending with 1 Square Knot on each side.

2 **Josephine Knot:** Using the 3 outer cords on each side, tie a Josephine Knot. Treat the 3 cords as one, keeping them side by side in the knot. Leave a ⅜" space above and below each Josephine Knot. (The 2 center cords go under the Josephine Knot.) Continue to repeat sections of Alternating Square Knots with Josephine Knots, until you have 5 Josephine Knots. End with a section of Square Knots.

3 Finish with a Double Overhand Knot. Trim the ends.

Eight Strand
Alternating
Square Knot

Josephine Knot

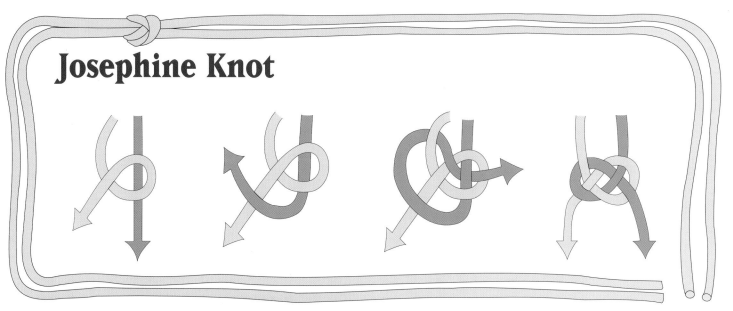

Simple Josephine Knot Choker

MATERIALS:
• One 90" piece of 2mm Natural hemp
INSTRUCTIONS:
1 Fold the cord in half; tie an Overhand Knot, leaving a ½" loop.
2 Tie 21 Josephine Knots, leaving a ½" space between each knot.
3 Finish with a Double Overhand Knot. Trim the ends.

Josephine Knot Choker with Large Bead

MATERIALS:
• One 100" piece of 2mm Natural hemp cord
• One large bead
INSTRUCTIONS:
1 Find the center of cord; tie an Overhand knot, leaving a ½" loop.
2 Tie 13 Josephine Knots, spacing them close together; add a bead onto both cords. Tie 13 Josephine Knots.
3 Finish with a Double Overhand Knot. Trim the ends.

Double Strand Josephine Knot Bracelet

MATERIALS:
• Two 200" pieces of 2mm Natural hemp cord
INSTRUCTIONS:
1 Fold the cords in half; tie an Overhand Knot, leaving a ½" loop.
2 Tie 13 Josephine Knots, spacing the knots close together. Treat the two cords as one, keeping them placed side by side as you shape the knot.
3 Finish with a Double Overhand Knot. Trim the ends.

Bauble Knot

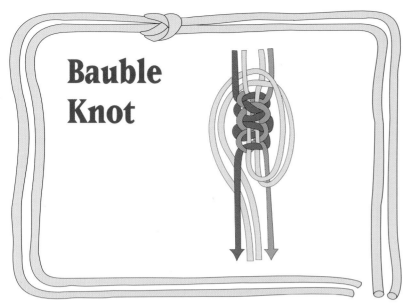

Lapis Bead Choker

MATERIALS:
• Four 120" pieces of 1mm Natural hemp
• Two square ¼" blue beads
• Three ½" blue nuggets

INSTRUCTIONS:
Fold the cords in half, tie an Overhand Knot, leaving a ½" loop.

1 Tie an Alternating Square Knot pattern (page 16) for 3½". Tie a Bauble Knot: With the 4 center cords, tie 3 Square Knots.

2 Take the filler cords, and bring them up to the space between the filler cords just above the first Square Knot. Thread through the center of filler cords (from front to back), and pull them back down with other cords.

3 Tie an Alternating Square Knot pattern for ½". Tie a Bauble Knot.

4 Separate cords into 2 groups, tie 1 Square Knot in each.

5 Add a square bead. Repeat Step 4. Tie a Bauble Knot. Repeat Step 4. Add 3 nugget beads. Repeat Step 4. Tie a Bauble Knot. Repeat Step 4. Add a square bead. Repeat Step 4. Tie a Bauble Knot. Tie an Alternating Square Knot pattern for ½". Tie a Bauble Knot.

6 Work an Alternating Square Knot pattern for 3½". Finish with a Double Overhand Knot. Trim the ends.

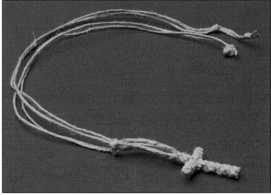

Knotted Cross

MATERIALS:
• Four 36" pieces of of 1mm Natural hemp
CROSS: See instruction on page 19
INSTRUCTIONS FOR NECKLACE:

1 Separate the 4 strands at the top of the cross into two groups; leave a 1" space, tie an Overhand Knot in each group.

2 On one end, leave a 7" space, tie an Overhand Knot, skip ½", tie an Overhand Knot. Trim the ends.

3 On the other end, leave a 7" space, tie a Double Overhand Knot. Trim the ends.

Helpful Hints
• To hold hemp in place tie knots, place strands on a foam block. Pin through the center of the first knot. Tie knots around the shaft of a T-pin.
• Stiffen the completed cross with a mixture of half water, half glue. Allow to dry thoroughly.